Body Talk

Break It Down

THE DIGESTIVE SYSTEM

Steve Parker

www.raintreepublishers.co.uk
Visit our website to find out more information about **Raintree** books.

To order:
☎ Phone 44 (0) 1865 888113
▤ Send a fax to 44 (0) 1865 314091
▢ Visit the Raintree bookshop at **www.raintreepublishers.co.uk**
to browse our catalogue and order online.

First published in Great Britain by Raintree, Halley Court, Jordan Hill, Oxford, OX2 8EJ, part of Harcourt Education.
Raintree is a registered trademark of Harcourt Education Ltd.

Editorial: Melanie Waldron, Rosie Gordon, and Megan Cotugno
Design: Philippa Jenkins, Lucy Owen, and John Walker
Illustrations: Darren Linguard and Jeff Edwards
Picture Research: Mica Brancic and Ginny Stroud-Lewis
Production: Chloe Bloom

Originated by Dot Gradations Ltd, UK
Printed and bound in China by South China Printing Company

10-digit ISBN: 1 406 20061 1
13-digit ISBN: 978 1 406 20061 4
10 09 08 07 06
10 9 8 7 6 5 4 3 2 1

British Library Cataloguing in Publication Data
Parker, Steve
    Break it down! : the digestive system. - (Body talk)   1.Digestion - Juvenile literature
2.Digestive organs -
    Juvenile literature
    I.Title
    612.3   ISBN-10: 1406200611
A full catalogue record for this book is available from the British Library.

Acknowledgements
The publishers would like to thank the following for permission to reproduce photographs: Alamy, **pp.** 7, 20-21; 12-13 (Bjorn Holland); Corbis **pp.** 6-7, 10-11, 14, 18-19, 37; **p.** 6 (Ariel Skelley), **p.** 15 (Gabe Palmer), **pp.** 40-41 (NASA/ Roger Ressmeyer), **p.** 12 (Steve Prezant), **p.** 43 (National Geographic/ Stephen Alvarez), **pp.** 8-9, 34-35 (PhotoDisc), **pp.** 16-17 (Taxi); Ginny Stroud-Lewis **p.** 9; Harcourt Education Ltd/Tudor Photograph **pp.** 23, 35; Science Photo Library **pp.**10; 35 (AJ Photo/ Hop Americain), **p.** 19 (BSIP), pp. 38-39 (BSIP VEM), **pp.** 22-23 (BSIP, VERO/Carlo), **pp.** 22, 29 (Eye Of Science), **p.** 28 (John Daugherty), **p.** 8 (Lawrence Lawry), **pp.** 24-25 (Manfred Kage), **pp.** 30-31 (Maximilian Stock Ltd), **pp.** 32-33 (Professors P. Motta & F. Carpino/ University "La Sapienza", Rome), **p.** 33 (Scotta Camazine), **pp.** 28-29 (Sinclair Stammers), **pp.** 26-27, 36-37 (Steve Gschmeissner), **p.** 31 (Vincent Zuber, Custom Medical Stock Photo), **p.** 36 (Zephyr); Superstock **pp.** 4-5, 12; 14-15, The Anthony Blake Photo Library/Sam Stowell **pp.** 14-15.

Cover photograph of man and apple reproduced with permission of Corbis/ LWA-Stephen Welstead.
The author and publisher would like to thank Ann Fullick for her assistance in the preparation of this book.

The paper used to print this book comes from sustainable resources.

Dedicated to the memory of Lucy Owen

Contents

Any words appearing in the text in bold, **like this**, are explained in the glossary. You can also look out for them in 'Body language' at the bottom of each page.

MMM – yummy!

Could you eat a pile of food bigger than a family car? You probably can, but it would take all year.

What would be your favourite food in that pile? Ice cream and chocolate, burger and fries, apples and pears, curry and rice, pasta and chicken ... even spinach and cabbage?

Many different kinds of foods are good for you and your body. Too much of one kind of food can be unhealthy, and boring too.

The incredible journey

After you swallow food, that seems like the end of it, until your next meal. But the food will go on an amazing journey through your body, travelling around nine metres and taking about 24 hours.

Mealtimes are a chance to ➤ catch up with family and friends, enjoy textures, tastes and flavours, and give the body the vital food it needs.

digest   break down something like food into smaller and smaller pieces
molecule   smallest part of a substance such as a nutrient in food

The big chunks of food will be crushed, mashed, attacked by acids, and gradually **digested** into tiny **molecules**. These will carried all around your body and get used in hundreds of different ways to keep you healthy, growing, on the move, and feeling good.

What is food for?

Nutrients from your food supply energy for your muscles to move, your heart to beat, your lungs to breathe, and your brain to think. Your food also provides substances for growing, mending your body's everyday wear and tear, and fighting off illness.

Apart from this, we love to eat! Many people like to sit with friends, chomp on a tasty meal, sip a delicious drink, and chat about the foods they love – and those they hate.

Find out later ...

How far can you run on an apple?

Where do your foods come from?

How long does food take to pass through you?

nutrient   useful substance in food that the body needs

What's made of food

What's the difference between fish and rice? Well, you don't often see fields of fish, or rice swimming in the sea! But food experts could add another answer. Fish contain lots of **proteins**, while rice has plenty of **carbohydrates**. Proteins and carbohydrates are two of the main groups of food substances that our bodies need.

Building the body

Your muscles and lots of other body parts are made of proteins. But they do not last forever. They gradually wear out and need replacing, by proteins from your food. You also need proteins from your food to grow and make your body parts bigger.

So proteins are "building foods". Meat, fish, eggs and dairy products like cheese are foods that contain a lot of protein. So do all sorts of beans, nuts and peas.

How much energy?

The energy in foods is used up by the body's activities, like running. Here is a rough guide to how far a person could run on the energy provided by some foods:

Apple	500 metres
Egg	1,000 metres
Slice of bread	1,200 metres
Portion of chicken	1,500 metres
Two scoops of ice-cream	2,500 metres
Bar of chocolate	3,500 metres
Packet of peanuts	4,300 metres

carbohydrates   starchy or sugary food substances that provide energy
energy   ability to cause changes and make things happen

Energy for life

Even when you sit still, your body uses **energy**, as your heart beats, your **guts** digest food and your whole body stays warm.

When you move about, your muscles use even more energy. This comes from food. Carbohydrates are "energy foods". They are often sweet-tasting, like bananas, or starchy, like potatoes. This is because sweet and starchy foods contain lots of carbohydrates.

Grains like wheat, rice and barley, and food made from them like bread and pasta, will give you lots of energy. So will vegetables and fruits like potatoes, bananas and sweetcorn. Chocolate, candies and sweets are high in carbohydrates too!

▼ Food doesn't simply appear on our plates. First it is grown, then harvested, transported and prepared. The food business is vast and needs huge areas of land to grow crops, like this giant wheat field.

DID YOU KNOW?

Food is fuel. It gives us energy, in the same way that petrol is fuel and provides energy for a car. If a person could get energy from petrol instead of food, one litre would be enough to run around 120 kilometres!

Younger, older

The food your body needs changes through your life. When you are young, you need plenty of protein foods for growing, like milk, eggs and cheese. You also need plenty of carbohydrate foods for rushing about and playing. Older people need less of these food groups.

guts   parts inside the lower body, such as the intestines
proteins   substances from food, used by the body for growth and healing

7

Added chemicals

Look at the labels on readymade foods like pizzas, pies and cakes. They may have chemical substances added to them:

✦ Colourings, to brighten the colour.

✦ Flavourings, to alter the taste.

✦ Preservatives, to help the food last longer.

But some of these can affect a person's behaviour or even make them feel ill or sick. In general – the fewer additives, the better.

The "F" foods

Have you ever eaten a fully fried meal? Fried bacon, fried eggs, fried mushrooms, fried fries ... maybe occasionally, but not every day. That wouldn't be healthy and can make you feel sick! Fried, greasy, oily foods contain lots of the substances known as **fats**. Like carbohydrates, fats provide the body with energy. Small amounts of fats are also needed so that body parts like nerves can work properly.

Not too much

Foods which contain lots of fats include red meats like beef and lamb, and especially processed meat foods like burgers and salamis. Milk, butter, eggs and dairy products contain fats. So do some plant foods like avocados, olives, peanuts and soya, and the oils made from them.

These foods all contain ➤ plenty of fibre, also known as roughage. Fibre keeps your guts working well.

What exactly are you eating?

blood vessels arteries, capillaries, and veins through which blood flows
constipation difficulty in getting rid of faeces or bowel movements

The problem is that too many fatty foods can be bad for the body, especially for the heart and **blood vessels**. In general, the oily fats from plants are healthier than the fatty fats from animal foods and products.

Just passing through

As well as fats, there is another important "F" substance that we need in foods – **fibre**. Oddly, the body does not digest it and take it in. Fibre passes through your body and comes out the other end, into the toilet.

But fibre helps to keep the insides of the **guts** working well, and it lessens the risk of some gut diseases. High-fibre foods include wholemeal or wholegrain breads, breakfast cereals and pastas. Fresh fruits and vegetables of most kinds, especially beans and peas, are also high in fibre.

FATTY FOODS ARE BAD FOODS!

A new report shows once again the dangers of eating too many fatty foods. Fat can be seen on fresh meat, and you can cut it off. But it is "hidden" in prepared foods like burgers, salamis, sausages and patés. Scientists think that too much can lead to diseases of the heart, blood vessels, bowels and liver.

Don't get stuck

Leftover food and other bits and pieces in the guts form waste material that the body does not need. Fibre in food is very important because it helps the waste to pass out of the body easily, into the toilet. Without plenty of fibre, the waste may get stuck inside us. This is called **constipation** and it is very uncomfortable!

fats food substances needed for energy and health, but which can damage the body if taken in large amounts
fibre food substances that are not digested, but help the guts work well

A pill a day

Lots of different foods, including fruits and vegetables, give us all the vitamins and minerals we need in a natural tasty form. We also get fibre and other needs from these foods. But some people like to chew a vitamin or mineral pill, just to make sure.

Extra-healthy!

Teeth are white. So is milk. So is the substance calcium. There is plenty of calcium in milk, and your body needs calcium for strong teeth (and strong bones too). Calcium is a food **mineral**. The body needs small amounts of many minerals, to work properly. Other minerals include iron for healthy blood, and magnesium for bones, muscles and nerves.

A terrible disease

Long ago, sailors on long sea voyages suffered from the terrible disease scurvy. They had sore lips, and bleeding gums, and their teeth fell out! Worse still, many become so weak that they died.

Scurvy was due to lack of fresh food, especially fresh fruits and vegetables. These foods contain plenty of substances called **vitamins**. As well as minerals, the body needs regular vitamins to stay healthy.

minerals   substances, such as iron, that the body needs to stay healthy

Vitamins have letters like A and B. Scurvy is cause by lack of vitamin C. This is found in citrus fruits like oranges and lemons, also green vegetables like cabbage and broccoli, green peppers, melons and tomatoes. Vitamin A is needed for healthy eyes, hair, skin and bones. It is found in fresh fruits and vegetables, fish and eggs.

A simple answer

The body needs about 13 vitamins and over 20 minerals. It would take hours to work out which foods provide the exact amounts. A better answer is to eat many different foods, especially fresh fruits and vegetables. Then you should get all the vitamins and minerals you need.

◄ Green for GO! These foods are very healthy, providing plenty of the minerals and vitamins we need every day. Which ones do you like best?

LIMEYS!

After it was discovered that fruit could prevent scurvy, in 1795 the British navy began to put stores of lime juice on all long sea voyages. British sailors stopped dying of scurvy, but picked up a new nickname that stuck – Limeys!

Five-a-day

The "five-a-day" guide means five pieces, portions, helpings or servings of fresh fruits or vegetables every day. So a banana, a meal with peas and carrots, some pineapple slices, and a crunchy apple would make up five. Of course, more than five is even better!

vitamin   food substance that the body needs to stay healthy

Problems of plenty

Being overweight, or obese, can affect the heart, blood vessels, muscles, bones, joints, guts, liver and many other body parts. It also makes exercise more difficult, which brings yet more risks. Obesity is a huge health problem in many countries.

Too much, too little

Millions of people around the world eat too much. They take in more food than their bodies need. Their bodies store the extra energy as body fat. This can make you overweight. Once you get too heavy or even **obese**, it can lead to many health problems.

Not enough

Yet also around the world, millions of people suffer for the opposite reason. They simply don't have enough to eat. Their bodies lack the important substances in food, such as carbohydrates for energy, proteins for body-building and repair, small amounts of fats, plenty of fibre, and regular supplies of vitamins and minerals. So while some people are ill from overeating, others starve to death.

I HAVEN'T TRIED THAT

Around the world, all kinds of things are eaten as food. What seems like a strange meal in one place is common in another. Here are some examples:

• Mosquito pie
• Fried grasshoppers
• Mashed seaweeds
• Inner parts of a starfish
• Possum droppings
• Blood sausage

Can you think of others?

Some plants and animals are ➤ raised for food in a natural way, without the use of chemicals and crowded farming methods. Many people prefer to eat such foods, which are often labelled "organic".

diet   what a person eats regularly
obese   overweight or "fat" enough to be unhealthy

Special diets

The range of foods that a person eats is called their **diet**. Some people like just about any food and have a "wide" diet. Others hold strong views which mean they avoid some foods. For instance, they might dislike the idea of animals being killed for food, so they avoid meat and animal products. This is a **vegetarian diet**. Or they might follow a certain faith or religion that teaches certain foods should not be eaten. Or they may be overweight, and so they eat less to lose unwanted body fat. This is a **reducing diet**.

Food at the centre

Foods do not just provide the body with nourishment. Sometimes a great event is based around a special meal. People come together to celebrate a birth, anniversary, wedding or special holiday (as below). For example, when do many people eat turkey?

reducing diet   consuming less energy than the body uses in order to lose weight
vegetarian diet   eating mainly or only foods from plants, and dairy produce

I'm hungry!

When was your last meal? Maybe you're not hungry at the moment. But think of your favourite food, how it smells and looks, and you might lick your lips! This shows how your thoughts and ideas can affect your wish for food, as well as your body's real needs.

Regular supplies

Our bodies are designed for food every few hours. So several meals through the day are best; usually one after waking up, one around midday, and one towards the end. Missing meals, especially breakfast, puts the body under stress and can make illness more likely.

Hunger signs

After some time without food, body parts like your muscles begin to run low on energy. Your blood carries sugar (glucose) around your body. It is the main source of energy for your **cells**. As you use **blood glucose**, its levels in your blood start to fall.

blood glucose sugar obtained from the breakdown of other sugars and carbohydrates in food. The main source of energy for the body.

Also your stomach and guts start to feel empty, since they have finished with the food from your last meal. Your brain recognizes all these signs, and you start to feel hungry.

Ready to eat

As soon as you smell and see food, your body gets ready to eat. One reaction that happens on its own, automatically, is that you get more **saliva** in your mouth. This makes you ready to chew the food into soft, wet, easy-to-swallow pieces. This is why we say a meal is "mouth-watering".

Food for thought

Your brain uses lots of energy all the time for thinking and other activities. If you don't eat regular meals, your energy-giving blood sugar may run low, and your brain can't get enough. Then you could feel dizzy, or "light-headed".

If you haven't eaten properly to get energy, you might not concentrate properly. Then even a fun activity like cycling can be more risky.

DID YOU KNOW?
You eat more than 12 times your body weight in food each year.

Tasty! Smelly too!

Often we don't realize how hungry we are until we sit down ready to eat. Then we look at the colours and shapes of the foods. We smell their wonderful odours as we prepare to take a bite. And we taste the fantastic flavours of the first few mouthfuls. Our senses of sight, smell and taste help us to enjoy our food.

Early warning

Yeuurrgh! Our senses also warn us about bad food. If it looks old or mouldy, or smells rotten, or tastes odd, then it may be no good for us. It could make us sick. Also, if we don't know what a food is, it could be poisonous, especially if it is picked from the wild. So our senses help us to enjoy food, and also protect us from harmful food.

Busy tongue

Your tongue is not just for tasting. It has many other uses. It moistens your lips so that they seal together as you chew, and bits don't fall out. It moves food around inside your mouth, from front to back and side to side. This lets you chew each mouthful properly. Your tongue also licks food off your lips. Try eating without licking your lips – it gets pretty messy!

bitter

sour

salty

sweet

Even before we taste a meal, ▶ our sense of smell tells us plenty. But it can also give odd messages. Some foods don't smell that good – yet they taste great.

salivary glands   six small glands around the mouth which make saliva
taste buds   ball-shaped groups of cells on the tongue which detect tastes

Spit, drool, dribble

Your **saliva** is a watery substance that helps to make foods soft and moist as you chew. It is made in six parts called **salivary glands**, under the skin around your mouth. These are just below and in front of each ear, under each side of your tongue, and inside each side of your lower jaw.

tongue

salivary glands

DID YOU KNOW?
Your salivary glands make more than one litre of saliva every day. That means you could take a bath in your own spit every two months!

17

Outside and inside

The outside of a tooth is an incredibly hard substance, **enamel**. Under this is **dentine**, which works like a cushion to lessen knocks and noise as you crunch tough foods. In the tooth's middle is **pulp**. It is mainly tiny blood vessels and the nerves that feel heat, cold, pressure, and the pain of toothache.

Terrific teeth

How many times each day do you bite and chew? Probably at least 3,000, and even more if you chew gum. That's a lot of work for your teeth. But teeth are your body's toughest parts, about five times harder than bone. For most people they last a lifetime as they nibble, gnaw, chew and munch.

A good start

The food you eat needs digesting – breaking down from big chunks into small molecules your body can take in and use. Your teeth begin the process of digestion. They chop your food into small pieces you can swallow.

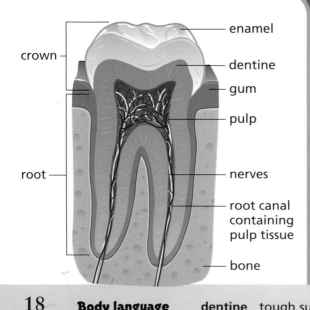

crown

root

- enamel
- dentine
- gum
- pulp
- nerves
- root canal containing pulp tissue
- bone

dentine   tough substance under tooth enamel
enamel   tough, whitish covering of the upper part of a tooth

Your teeth also squash and mash hard foods so they are soft and easier to swallow. The more you chew, the better your digestion, and the more goodness and nourishment you get.

How many teeth?

Another question about teeth – how many do you have? It depends partly on how old (or young) you are. New babies have almost none. By the age of about three you probably had all 20 of your first "baby" teeth. Then these fall out naturally, and over the next ten years or so, your permanent adult teeth grow. There are usually 32 of these teeth. But in some people the last of these may never grow. Or they might get too crowded, so the dentist takes away a few.

◄ Once your adult teeth come through, you need to care for them properly. The dentist will tell you how to keep this new set for life!

GOOD FOR TEETH
- Brushing every day with a fluoride toothpaste, preferably after each meal and before bed.
- Careful flossing between teeth with a thin thread.
- Visiting the dentist every 6 or 12 months.

BAD FOR TEETH
- No brushing, flossing or dental checks.
- Eating lots of sweet or sugary foods.

My friend the dentist

Some people boast they haven't seen the dentist for years. Then they feel slight discomfort in their teeth, which gets worse, and turns into toothache, which really hurts. This means lots of dental work, and fillings, or even false teeth! It is much better to have a regular check-up.

This dental X-ray ▲ shows tooth decay (caries), a hole (cavity), and a filling.

Down the hatch

As you chew a mouthful of food, it turns into a mushy soup. This part of food's digestion is physical – squeezing and squashing. But there is another type of digestion that is less easy to see. This is chemical digestion.

On the attack

Chemical digestion begins with a special substance in your saliva, called **amylase**. It breaks down the starchy parts of your food such as rice, bread and potatoes, and makes them into smaller molecules, mainly sugars.

If you keep chewing a mouthful of bread, you might slowly begin to taste sweetness that wasn't there at first. This is amylase at work, turning starch to sugar.

Amylase is the first of many natural chemicals, called **digestive enzymes**, which attack the food on its journey through the body.

Soft and slippery

Chewing also makes food soft and slippery, so it slides down easily when you swallow. Swallowing is an automatic body **reflex** that you hardly think about. But try it slowly. Feel what happens at each stage, inside your mouth and throat, and with your hand on your neck. Can you feel the process as it is shown in these diagrams?

Gulp!

✦ Your tongue pushes a small lump of food back into your throat.

✦ The lump goes down past the top of your **windpipe**.

✦ The windpipe's top closes to stop food going the "wrong way" into it, which would cause choking.

✦ The lump goes into your food-pipe or **gullet**, down through your neck and chest, into your stomach.

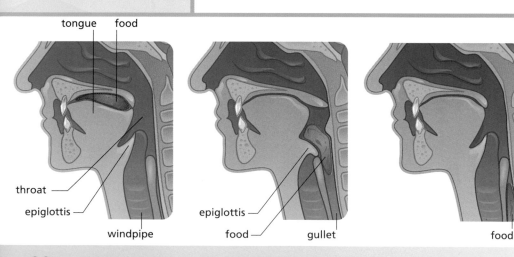

tongue   food

throat

epiglottis

windpipe

epiglottis

food   gullet

food

You might swallow food the "wrong way" into your **windpipe**, and choke, if you:

✦ rush your food and eat too quickly
✦ talk while eating
✦ eat while trying to do something else like walking or running.

It is best sit quietly, chewing with your mouth closed. That way you can enjoy the taste and swallow safely, without dribbling.

◄ Spaghetti goes into your mouth as long worm-like strings. But after chewing, it is swallowed into your gullet as mashed-up lumps.

reflex automatic reaction like blinking or coughing

stomach and guts

Acids are dangerous chemicals. They can burn skin, so they are kept in safe jars or containers. Yet there is a strong acid in your body right now! It is in your stomach and it is called **hydrochloric acid**. It is an important part of **gastric juice** – the slimy, sticky substance made by the inside of your stomach.

Chemicals that kill

Powerful chemicals in gastric juice break apart the food you swallow. As well as acid, there are also protein-digesting **enzymes** in your stomach. These work like the amylase in your saliva, but they break down other substances too, like proteins, into smaller molecules.

This combination of acid and enzymes is lethal. Gastric juice usually kills any germs that came in by accident with your food and drink!

Into a soup

When food squelches into your stomach, it is passing through your **digestive tract**. This tract is the passageway for food all through your body, from your mouth to the bottom end. As well as attacking food with chemicals, your stomach has strong muscles in its walls. These make it squirm and writhe like a fat worm, to squeeze and stir the food into a thick, sloppy soup.

Self-defence

The stomach wall has thousands of tiny blobs called **glands**. These make acids and enzymes for the gastric juice. They also make a thick slime called mucus, which covers the stomach's inside and protects it from gastric juices. Otherwise the stomach would digest itself!

The stomach wall has micro-pits, where gastric juice is made.

The stomach is not behind the ➤ bellybutton as many people think. It is higher and to one side, under the lower left ribs.

Body language   enzyme   substance that controls the speed of chemical change, such as digestion

TIMELINE OF DIGESTION

This is how long a lump of food stays in each part:

Mouth	Up to 1 minute
Gullet	2-5 seconds
Stomach	2-5 hours
Small intestine	1-4 hours
Large intestine	10-18 hours

stomach

large intestine

small intestine

Uuuuuuurgh!

The stomach normally holds up to 1.5 litres. But if we eat too much, our bodies may get rid of some food by pushing it back up the way it came. This is being sick, also known as throwing up or vomiting. The muscles around the stomach and gullet are so powerful that they can hurl vomit out of the mouth more than three metres!

glands   parts that make and release a substance such as acid, spit, or sweat

Narrow but long

Imagine putting a whole meal into a food blender and whizzing it for a few minutes. No matter what went in, it probably ends up as a brown mush. Your digestive parts do the same to the food you eat. A few hours after eating a beautiful, delicious meal, your stomach has turned it into a sloppy, dark soup. This is ready for the next part of the food's journey – into the **intestines**.

Smaller

After your stomach comes your small intestine. It is "small" because it is only slightly wider than your thumb. But it is very long, and coiled inside your body like a hosepipe. Food is squeezed into it from the stomach.

There are lots of different **enzymes** and chemicals in your small intestine. In fact, this is where most digestion takes place. After your food has been broken down in your small intestine, the final products, small food **molecules** such as glucose, are taken into your body.

Pushing food

Food does not slide through your gullet, stomach and intestines by itself. Their muscles push it along (shown below). The muscles tighten in waves to make the food inside ooze along. This is called **peristalsis**. It is so strong that you could eat food standing on your head! But don't try - you might choke or be sick.

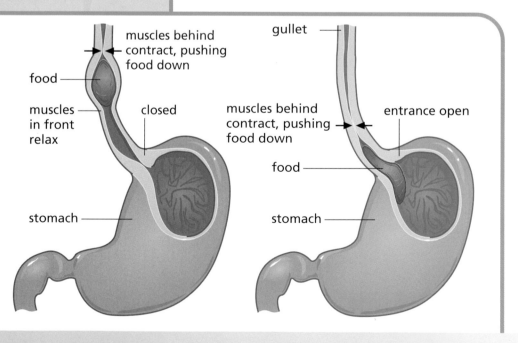

muscles behind contract, pushing food down

food

muscles in front relax

closed

gullet

muscles behind contract, pushing food down

entrance open

food

stomach

stomach

intestine   long digestive parts called guts or bowels, after the stomach
peristalsis   muscle contractions in body parts that move their contents along

Larger

Following your small intestine is the larger one. It is "large" because it is quite wide, almost the width of your hand. But it is only one-quarter as long as the small intestine. Its main tasks are to take in a few final **nutrients** from the digested food, and to soak up most of the water from it. This leaves the wastes as squishy, smelly, brown lumps. What happens to these? We will see later ...

Straightened out

Your whole **digestive tract** is around nine metres long. The longest part is the small intestine, at six metres. Luckily it is bent and folded many times, like a tangle of string. If your digestive parts were all straight, you would need to be six times taller than you are now!

▲ This is a "foods-eye view" as it moves from the stomach into the pipe–like small intestine.

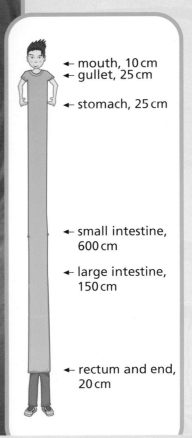

← mouth, 10 cm
← gullet, 25 cm

← stomach, 25 cm

← small intestine, 600 cm

← large intestine, 150 cm

← rectum and end, 20 cm

Soft and floppy

The pancreas is a long, pink, soft, floppy, wedge-shaped part just behind your stomach. Its juices pass along a short tube, the **pancreatic duct**, to the small intestine. Its hormones pass straight into the blood flowing through it.

Powerful juices

When did you last throw up? Can you recall a horrible bitter taste in your mouth? This is due mainly to your stomach juices. But it is not only your stomach that makes powerful chemicals to break down and digest food. Your **pancreas** also does this. It is just behind your stomach. Pancreas juices flow along a short tube into the small intestine. The juices contain more than 12 of the strong chemicals called enzymes. In the small intestine, these different enzymes break apart different parts of food, like proteins, starches and fats.

liver

stomach

pancreatic
duct

pancreas

glucagon   hormone that raises blood glucose
hormones   substances made by glands that affect of control the way
    various parts work

Two-timer

But the pancreas is a two-timer. It has another task. In addition to making digestive juices, it produces substances called **hormones**. These travel around in the blood and control the way various body parts work.

The pancreas makes two hormones, called **insulin** and **glucagon**. They control the amount of glucose sugar in the blood, which the body uses for energy. Insulin lessens blood sugar, while glucagon increases it. So the pancreas helps to take in sugar by digestion, and also control its amount in the blood.

Problem pancreas

In some people, the pancreas does not make its hormones, especially insulin. Or the insulin does not work properly. This means blood sugar levels go too high or too low, which can cause problems around the body. This condition is called **diabetes**. People with diabetes may have to get the insulin they need by injection.

◄ The pancreas contains about one million tiny blobs called islets. These make hormones to control blood sugar. The parts around them (called acini) make digestive juices.

JUICY THREE

The pancreas makes about 1.5 litres of digestive juices each day, which happens to be about the same amount of saliva and stomach juices produced by the mouth and the stomach.

insulin   hormone that lowers blood glucose levels

More juices

The liver's digestive juice is a thick yellow-green liquid called **bile**. It is stored in a small bag just under the liver, the gall bladder. As you eat, bile flows along a tube into the small intestine. Bile helps your enzymes digest the fats in your food.

Inside at last

Strange as it may seem, when you swallow food, it is not really "inside" your body. The digestive passageway is like a hollow tube through the body. Food only gets truly inside the body when it is digested into the tiny molecules. These pass through the walls of the digestive passageway and into the body. This happens in the longest part of the tube, the small intestine.

Hairy guts

If you could stroke the inside of a small intestine, it would feel velvety, like a soft rug or carpet. This is because it has about 500 million tiny "hairs", each less than one millimetre long. They are called **villi**. Joined end to end they would stretch over 400 kilometres! Inside each one are even tinier blood vessels.

Plenty of juices

Food in the small intestine is swimming in digestive juices. They came from saliva, the stomach, the pancreas, the small intestine itself, and also from the **liver**, just above the intestine. Nutrients are broken down into their tiniest forms, and these are small enough to pass easily into the blood inside the tiny villi of the small intestine. Then the blood carries away the nutrients and spreads them around the body.

gall bladder

bile duct

pancreas

small intestine

If your body was see-through, ➤ you could see the mushy, part-digested food from your last meal inside – just like the gut contents of this transparent jellyfish!

bile digestive juice made by the liver that flows to the small intestine
liver large organ that adjusts levels of vitamins, minerals and blood glucose, and carries out many other tasks

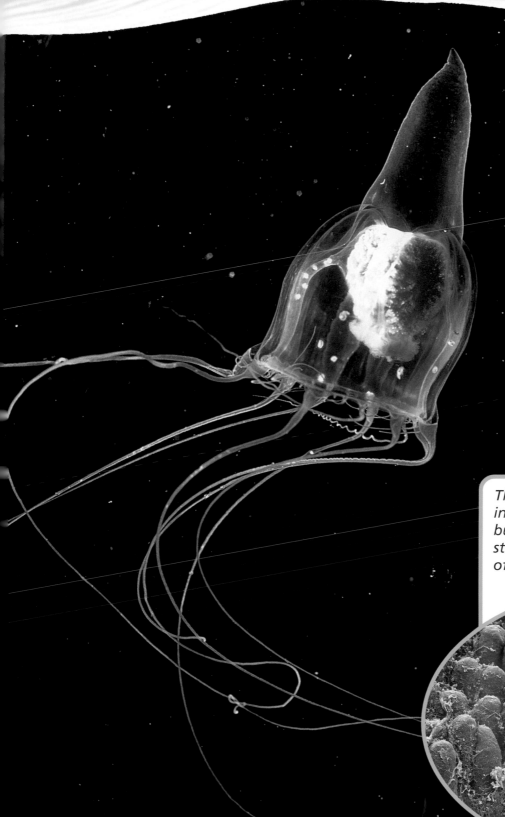

More and more

The tiny villi in the small intestine make its lining much bigger in area, compared to a flat lining. Also each one is covered with around 5,000 even tinier "hairs" called microvilli. These increase the area even more. The inner surface of a small intestine, spread out flat, would cover over three school classrooms!

The villi of the small intestine lining look like bunches of tiny fingers, sticking into the "soup" of digested food.

villi tiny hair-like parts lining the small intestine, which absorb nutrients

Blood red liver

Your liver is shaped like a curved triangle, just behind your lower right ribs. It is made of thousands of tiny six-sided lumps called lobules, each as big as a pinhead. The whole liver is dark red because it has so much blood inside.

liver

stomach

gall bladder

lobules

Major multi-tasker

Can you multi-task? This means thinking about, and doing, several things at once. Your liver certainly can. It has more than 500 tasks! After your skin, it is your second largest **organ**, and the body's largest gland. And it is so busy with nutrients and body chemicals that, as you rest after a big meal, it produces up to one-fifth of all your body warmth.

Making, changing, storing

Most of the liver's tasks involve dealing with nutrients from digested food. These nutrients come straight to the liver in the blood from the small intestine. As they arrive, the liver sets to work. It breaks down some of the nutrients into smaller pieces.

A massive chemical factory ➤ produces dozens of substances, but your liver does far more, and in a much smaller space.

EXCUSE ME ...
As we eat, especially if we rush, we often swallow air. Also there is gas in fizzy drink bubbles. This gas and air usually come back up from the stomach as a belch or burp.

jaundice yellowing of skin or eyes usually due to a liver problem
organ main body part, like brain, heart, liver, or intestine

These can be used by the body more easily. It stores some, especially certain vitamins and minerals, in case supplies are lacking in your next meals. Also the liver is the main place where harmful substances like alcohol and **toxins** are made harmless. This is called detoxifying or "detox".

Up and down

If sugar in the blood is high, the liver joins together sugars to make body starch, which it stores for later. If blood sugar runs low, the liver breaks down its starch into sugar, which it lets go into the blood. The liver also makes bile to help with digestion. And it does lots, lots more!

Turning yellow

One of the liver's tasks is to get rid of old, worn-out **red blood cells**. If the liver is harmed by injury or illness, the colouring substance from old red cells builds up in the blood. It gradually turns the skin and the whites of the eyes yellow. This condition is called **jaundice**.

... PARDON!

The chemical changes of digestion make gas bubbles. These make gurgling "stomach rumbles" inside our intestines. This gas comes out of the bottom end as a ... what would you call it?

red blood cells cells in the blood which carry oxygen around the body
toxin harmful or poisonous chemical or substance

W ut n t? W st it!

Out at last

The large intestine, or **colon**, makes solid wastes into soft brown lumps. These are stored in the end part, the **rectum**. Finally, when the time is right, the lumps are squeezed through of a ring of muscle at the end called the anus, and down the toilet.

Your body takes in a big pile of food each year – over half a tonne. It also takes in plenty of drinks; more than seven bathtubs-full. All of this does not stay inside, otherwise you would be a giant! Unused parts of food, as well as old, worn-out body bits, come out in two main forms:

• One form is solid wastes, also known as bowel motions, excrement or faeces. They are called plenty of other names, too!

• The other form is liquid wastes, also called urine, and sometimes 'water', although it is not just water, of course. Liquid wastes are called many other names too!

These two types of wastes are formed in very different ways, by different parts of the body.

colon
appendix   anus
rectum

bacteria   microscopic organisms of many types
colon   another name for the large intestine

Solids out

Solid wastes come out of the end of the digestive passageway. They are not only leftover food, or parts of food that cannot be digested, like fibre. Leftovers and fibre form less than one-fifth of solid wastes. About the same amount again is lining of the stomach and intestines, rubbed off as food passes through. And a similar amount is made up of certain types of **microbes**, called **bacteria**! These are our natural friends. They live in our insides all the time, mainly in the large intestine. Billions of them help digestion and your gut to work properly. The rest of the solid wastes, sometimes up to half, is water.

▼ In your guts live billions of microbes, mainly bacteria (sausage-shaped in this picture). There are enough to fill three cups.

Danger... or just passing through?

Any swallowed hard object can cause serious problems. It may get stuck in the digestive tube and block food, or poke through the lining and cause damage. This is why we keep small items like beads and pins away from babies and young children.

If a swallowed object is small and smooth, like a ring or marble, it may pass right through and out the other end. If not, it will need an urgent visit to hospital.

microbes   tiny living things, which can only be seen under a microscope
rectum   store for waste before it passes out through the anus

33

Total control

Making urine

Urine is made in your kidneys, which are found behind your liver and stomach. They filter your blood and make urine all the time. The urine leaves your kidneys and trickles down tubes called **ureters** to your **bladder**. Your bladder stores the urine until you go to the toilet. Then another tube, called the urethra, takes the urine to the outside of your body.

Watery wastes

Each time you get rid of liquid waste, it is not really much to do with digestion. Urine is very different from solid waste. It does not come directly from leftover food in the stomach and guts.

If you eat too much **protein**, it has to be broken down in your liver before you can use it. The same is true for the old cells that your body no longer needs. Your liver produces a poisonous waste called urea from all this protein breakdown, and the urea goes into your blood.

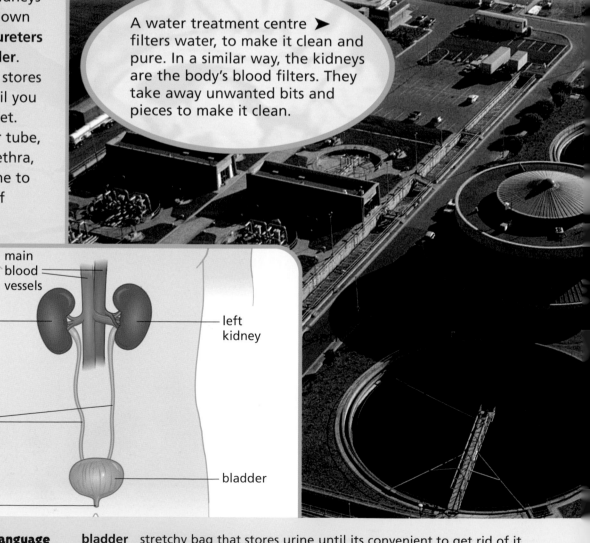

A water treatment centre ➤ filters water, to make it clean and pure. In a similar way, the kidneys are the body's blood filters. They take away unwanted bits and pieces to make it clean.

main blood vessels

right kidney

left kidney

ureters

bladder

urethra

bladder   stretchy bag that stores urine until its convenient to get rid of it
ureter   tube that carries urine from each kidney to the bladder

Where wastes are removed

Your blood carries digested food **molecules** to the billions of cells in your body where they are used for energy and as building materials. It also takes away the unwanted waste, including urea. On every journey around your body, your blood flows through your two kidneys. This is where the urea is removed. Your kidneys also balance the amount of water and body salts and minerals in your blood. You can find out how they work on pages 36-37.

The most blood

The kidneys receive far more blood than any other body part, for their size. They weigh only 1/200th of the whole body, yet they take almost one-fifth of all the blood pumped out from the heart. This means your blood passes through your kidneys more than 300 times each day!

LIFE-SAVER

Some people have kidney disease, when wastes build up in their blood. A process called **renal dialysis** can help. The person's blood passes along a tube to an "artificial kidney machine", a dialysis machine. This does the kidney's job of filtering the blood, which then flows along another tube back to the body.

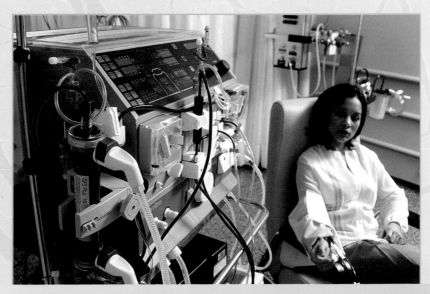

renal dialysis   using an "artificial kidney machine" to clean blood, when somebody's kidneys are not working properly

Cleaning the blood

By the time food has been digested, taken into the body, altered by the liver, carried around in the blood, and used by billions of microscopic cells, most of its nutrients have changed. Gone are the large molecules of proteins, fats and carbohydrates. Their breakdown is complete.

The small molecules that are produced are built into new materials by your body. And some of them are broken down to give waste products like urea. If too much urea collects in your blood, it will poison you, so it must be removed. This is the task of the kidneys.

In some people, hard stony material collects in the centre of a kidney, where urine should be. This forms a **kidney stone** (like the one below). It can be cut out during an operation. Or it can be shattered into tiny pieces by powerful high-pitched sound waves, called ultrasound. The tiny bits flow away with urine.

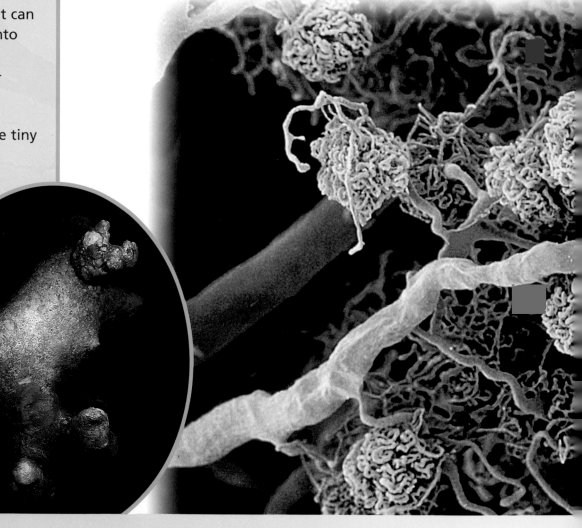

kidney stone hard object that can form in the kidney
nephron microscopic filtering unit inside the kidney

Million micro-filters

Inside each kidney, the blood passes through more than one million micro-filters, which are called **nephrons**. Each has a tangle of tiny blood vessels and other tubes. The nephrons take out wastes and unwanted substances from the blood, along with any water which your body does not need. The water and wastes together form urine. The urine collects in a space at the centre of the kidney. From here it flows slowly down a tube, the **ureter**, to be stored in the **bladder**.

▼ Each knot of tiny blood vessels is part of one micro-filter in the kidney. Unwanted wastes are squeezed out of the knot, into the space around it, where they start to form urine.

Night-time shutdown

The kidneys work fast all day. But at night, when you sleep, they work much slower, and make less urine. This is very helpful. It means you don't have to keep getting up through the night to use the toilet!

DID YOU KNOW?

The kidney's million micro-filters have very thin tubes, but they are very long too. If you could join all these tiny tubes from one kidney end-to-end, they would stretch almost 100 kilometres!

I'll burst!

Some people say: "I must get to the toilet or I'll burst!" But a burst bladder is very, very rare. Usually, when we can hold on no longer, we simply have to let out the urine. So it is a good idea to find a toilet well before this happens!

Weeeeeee!

When did you last get rid of your urine? And when do you think you may have to go again? Many people get rid of urine 10 or more times each day. It is called **urinating**, peeing, weeing ... and many other things! The bladder, which stores the urine, is the shape of a pear. When empty, it is not much bigger than your thumb. As it fills with urine, it blows up like a balloon filling with water.

The need to go

As the bladder fills, tiny **sensors** in its wall detect the amount of stretch, and tell the brain. Most people feel a slight urge to urinate when the bladder holds 250-300 millilitres – about the amount in a coffee mug. By 400-500 millilitres, the urge is much stronger. By 500-600 millilitres the need is desperate!

sensor   part which detects something, like sound, or the level of a substance inside itself, and sends messages to the brain

Letting it out

To let out urine, a ring of muscles around the start of the **urethra** tube goes loose and relaxes. Then muscles in the bladder wall tighten to make the whole bladder shrink, like pressing on a balloon. If you try to hold on too long, or try to pass urine too quickly, you may strain these muscles. It is best to use the toilet earlier rather than later, and take all the time you need.

Does colour matter?

Urine is usually a pale yellow colour. But if the body gets very hot, it loses water as sweat. So there is less water to go into urine, but the same amount of colour, making the urine darker yellow. Some foods have colours in them that pass into urine. Beetroot turns it red!

◄ This computer-coloured x-ray shows urine partly filling the bladder, which is nestling in the bowl-like base of the pelvis.

urethra   tube that takes urine from the bladder to outside the body

All "under control"

Hungry, thirsty

When your energy levels of blood sugar run too low, you feel hungry. And when your body detects it does not have enough water, you are thirsty. These feelings happen in a tiny part of your brain called your **hypothalamus**. The feelings can become so strong that you think of nothing else!

Every day you eat and enjoy your foods, gulp down delicious drinks, and then forget about them. But inside you, the processes of digestion and getting rid of wastes are very complicated. Lots of different body parts need to work together, each at the right time. You are probably not aware of any of this. Your brain controls all these processes automatically, so you don't have to think about them.

Electricity and chemicals

Your body is controlled in two main ways. One way is by sending out messages from the brain along **nerves** to the various body parts. The messages are in the form of tiny electrical signals.

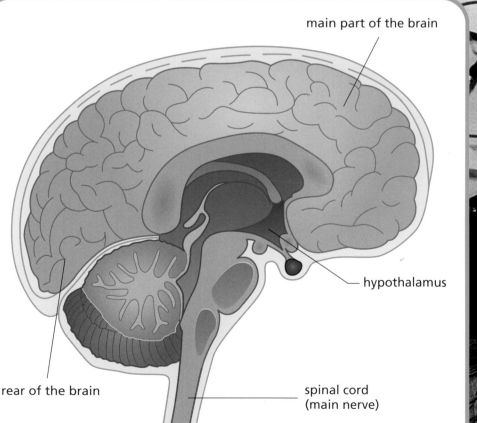

main part of the brain

hypothalamus

rear of the brain

spinal cord
(main nerve)

hypothalamas   small area at the front of the brain that deals with strong feelings, and automatic processes like body temperature

The other way is by natural body chemicals called **hormones**. These are made by parts called hormone-making or endocrine glands, as well as by the stomach, intestines and kidneys.

Together the hormones and nerve messages make sure digestion and getting rid of wastes happen properly. Rarely, something goes wrong. Then you might be sick, or feel pain due to germs in food, or race to the toilet because the wastes are coming out too soon!

▼ The body's digestion works normally inside, even when the surroundings are very unusual outside - like floating weightless in a space station!

LET'S WORK TOGETHER

Here are some of your digestive hormones and what they do.

Hormone	Made in	What it does
Gastrin	Stomach	Releases stomach juices
Secretin	Small intestine	Releases pancreas juices
CCK	Small intestine	Releases bile from gall bladder

DID YOU KNOW?

"Hunger pains" or "stomach pangs" happen several hours after your last proper meal. They are due to the stomach and intestines starting to churn and writhe again, because they expect your next meal. If you haven't eaten, you feel the movements because the stomach and intestines are empty.

nerves   string-like parts that carry messages around the body as tiny pulses of electricity

Water in foods

Your food provides more than a quarter of the water you need. Some foods are more watery than others (see table below).

I'm thirsty

About two-thirds of your body is water. If it was taken out, there would be enough for someone to take two or three showers. But of course, life cannot carry on without water. It is vital for every body part. Your blood is over four-fifths water, your brain three-quarters water, and even your bones are one-fifth water. An average person needs more than two litres of water every day to stay healthy. This is because all the nutrients, hormones, chemicals and other substances inside the body can only move about and change if they are "floating" in water. Without it, body changes would stop – dead.

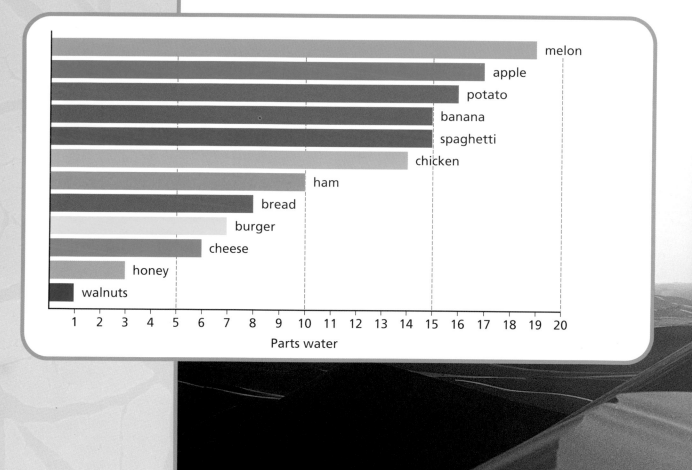

Parts water

Where body water comes from

- Most people need about one and a half litres of water each day as drinks. A typical drink like cola, lemonade, tea or coffee is almost all water. But the best drink is pure water.

- About three-quarters of a litre of water is inside foods, from a juicy melon to hard, dry nuts or biscuits.

- The body also makes its own water inside. Some of its inner chemical changes actually produce water – about one-third of a litre every day.

Foods, drinks and you

Water in a drink washes down your meal. It helps you to taste, chew and swallow the food. It also helps you to break down the food and digest the nutrients in your stomach and guts. This is how you look after your body, by eating healthy foods and sipping the right drinks. Food helps the body to grow and work properly – but first, you must break it down!

Recycling

Your digestion and waste systems make many juices in saliva, the stomach, pancreas and liver. They filter lots of wastes from the blood. Yet they take back almost all of the water from these juices and wastes. If they didn't, you would have to drink more than 100 times more water than you usually drink. And you would be using the toilet for more than two hours every day!

◀ Don't ignore thirst! By the time your brain says you are thirsty, your body already needs water. It works better with drinks little and often, rather than a few huge gulps all at once.

Find out more

The Natural History Museum in London has a human biology gallery. There, you can hear what a baby hears in the womb, see how bones and muscles work together, and find out all about the amazing human body.

Natural History Museum, Cromwell Road, London, SW7 5BD

www.nhm.ac.uk

Books

The Digestive System, Carol Ballard (Heinemann Library, 2003)

Guts: Our Digestive System, Seymour Simon 2005 (Harper Collins, 2005)

Our Bodies: Digestion, Steve Parker (Hodder Wayland, 2005)

Body: An Amazing Tour of Human Anatomy, Robert Winston (Dorling Kindersley, 2005)

World Wide Web

If you want to find out more about the stomach and digestion, you can search the Internet using keywords like these:

- 'small intestine'
- saliva + digestion
- kidney stones

You can also find your own keywords by using headings or words from this book. Use the search tips opposite to help you find the most useful websites.

Search tips

There are billions of pages on the Internet so it can be difficult to find exactly what you are looking for. For example, if you just type in 'water' on a search engine like Google, you will get a list of 19 million web pages. These search skills will help you find useful websites more quickly:

- Use simple keywords instead of whole sentences
- Use two to six keywords in a search, putting the most important words first
- Be precise – only use names of people, places or things
- If you want to find words that go together, put quote marks around them, for example 'stomach acid' or 'length of intestine'
- Use the advanced section of your search engine
- Use the + sign between keywords to link them, for example typing + KS3 after your keyword will help you find web pages at the right level.

Where to search

Search engine

A search engine looks through the entire web and lists all sites that match the words in the search box. It can give thousands of links, but the best matches are at the top of the list, on the first page. Try **bbc.co.uk/search**

Search directory

A search directory is like a library of websites that have been sorted by a person instead of a computer. You can search by keyword or subject and browse through the different sites like you look through books on a library shelf. A good example is **yahooligans.com**

Glossary

amylase enzyme in saliva that starts the breakdown of carbohydrates (sugars and starches) in food

bacteria organisms of many types

bile digestive juice made by the liver that flows to the small intestine

bladder stretchy bag that stores urine until it is convenient to get rid of it

blood glucose sugar obtained from the breakdown of other sugars and carbohydrates in food. The main source of energy for the body.

blood vessels arteries, capillaries, and veins through which blood flows

carbohydrates starchy or sugary food substances that provide energy

cells microscopic "building blocks" which make up all body parts

colon name for the large intestine

constipation difficulty in getting rid of faeces or bowel movements

dentine tough substance under tooth enamel

diabetes when insulin is not made or doesn't work, so blood glucose is not controlled

diet what a person eats regularly

digest break down something like food into smaller and smaller pieces

digestive enzymes chemicals that break food down in digestion

digestive tract parts that food passes through, from mouth to anus

enamel tough, whitish covering of the upper part of a tooth

energy ability to cause changes and make things happen

enzyme substance that controls the speed of a chemical change, such as digestion

fats food substances needed for energy, but which can damage the body if taken in large amounts

fibre food substances that are not digested, but help the guts work well

gastric juice mixture of hydrochloric acid and enzymes made by stomach lining to digest food

glands parts that make and release a substance, such as acid, spit, or sweat

glucagon hormone that raises blood glucose

gullet also called the oesophagus, tube from the throat to the stomach

guts parts inside the lower body, such as the intestines

hormones substances made by glands that affect the way various parts work

hydrochloric acid powerful digestive chemical made by the stomach lining

hypothalamus small area at the front of the brain that deals with strong feelings, and automatic processes like body temperature

insulin hormone that lowers blood glucose levels

intestines long digestive parts after the stomach

jaundice yellowing of the skin and eyes, usually due to a liver problem

kidney stone hard object that can form in the kidney

liver large organ that adjusts levels of vitamins, minerals, and blood glucose, and carries out many other tasks

microbes tiny living things, which can only be seen under a microscope

minerals substances, such as iron, the body needs to stay healthy

molecule smallest piece of a substance, such as a nutrient in food

nephron microscopic filtering unit inside the kidney

nerves string-like parts that carry messages around the body as tiny pulses of electricity

nutrients useful substances in food that the body needs

obese overweight or "fat" enough to be unhealthy

organ main body part, like brain, heart, liver, or intestine.

pancreas part that makes juices for digestion and hormones to control the level of blood glucose

pancreatic duct tube for pancreatic juices, from the pancreas to the small intestine

peristalsis muscle contractions of body parts that move their contents along

proteins substances from foods, used by the body for growth and healing

pulp soft substance in the middle of a tooth, containing blood vessels and nerve endings

rectum store for waste before it passes out through the anus

red blood cells cells in the blood which carry oxygen around the body

reducing diet consuming less energy than the body uses, in order to lose weight

reflex automatic reaction like blinking or coughing

renal dialysis using an "artificial kidney machine" to clean blood, when a person's kidneys do not work properly

saliva watery substance, also called spit, that makes food easier to swallow

salivary glands six small glands around the mouth which make saliva

sensor part which detects something, like sound, or the level of a substance inside itself, and sends messages to the brain

taste buds ball-shaped groups of cells on the tongue which detect tastes

toxin harmful or poisonous chemical or substance

ureter tube that carries urine from each kidney to the bladder

urethra tube that takes urine from the bladder to outside the body

urinating Getting rid of urine from the bladder to outside the body

vegetarian diet eating mainly or only food from plants, and dairy produce

villi tiny hair-like parts lining the small intestine, which absorb nutrients

vitamins food substances the body needs to stay healthy

windpipe tube, also called the trachea, which carries air between the throat and lungs when breathing

Inde

Titles in the *Body Talk* series include:

Hardback   1 4062 0062 X

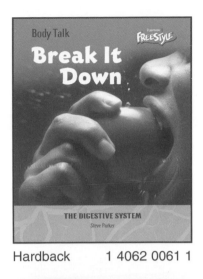

Hardback   1 4062 0061 1

Hardback   1 4062 0065 4

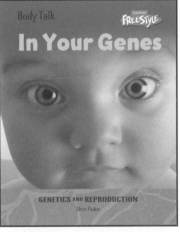

Hardback   1 4062 0063 8

Hardback   1 4062 0066 2

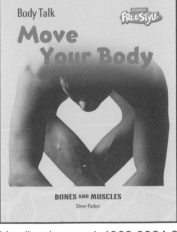

Hardback   1 4062 0064 6

Find out about the other titles in this series on our website www.raintreepublishers.co.uk